Original title:

Quivered Tones Under the Mermaid Puff

Author: Paula Raudsepp

ISBN HARDBACK: 978-1-80562-427-1

ISBN PAPERBACK: 978-1-80563-948-0

Ocean's Caress: A Whispered Saga

Beneath the waves, a secret lies,
A tapestry the sea supplies.
With salty air and secrets spun,
The ocean's song has just begun.

Whispers of tales from ages past,
Where dreams take form, they hold steadfast.
In shadows deep and colors bright,
The ebbing tide reveals the light.

Mermaids dance on coral reefs,
While sailors weave their wild beliefs.
The moonbeams kiss the ocean's face,
In nature's thrall, we find our place.

Each ripple tells a tale untold,
Of journeys bold, and hearts of gold.
The ocean's caress, a gentle muse,
Our spirits lifted, we cannot refuse.

So listen close, let magic swell,
For in its depths, a million spells.
The whispered saga calls to thee,
In every wave, a mystery.

Tales from the White-Flecked Tide

The tide recedes, revealing dreams,
In fragments lost like twinkling beams.
Upon the shore, footprints align,
Of seekers bold, in fate's design.

Seagulls cry their ragged tune,
As twilight dances with the moon.
Each grain of sand, a story spun,
Of fleeting love, and battles won.

Waves crash forth with ancient might,
Unfurling tales of day and night.
Whispers ride the ocean's breath,
Entwined with life, and secrets, death.

In every swell, in every foam,
There lies a heart, there lies a home.
The white-flecked tide, a canvas vast,
Paints histories, forever cast.

Each tide that comes, each tide that goes,
Each story washed, yet never slows.
So let us gather, hand in hand,
And weave our tales upon the sand.

Glistening Notes from the Deep's Heart

In the depths where shadows play,
Glistening notes begin to sway,
Whispers of the ocean's breath,
Songs that rise even from death.

Bubbles dance in liquid grace,
Treasures hidden, time can't erase,
Echoes of a siren's tune,
Underneath the watchful moon.

Coral reefs, a vibrant crowd,
Sing together, clear and loud,
Each note a shimmer on the tide,
Secrets in the sea that hide.

Fins like silver, swift and bright,
Sketching arcs in soft moonlight,
Melodies of ancient lore,
Calling forth what came before.

In this world, where dreams take flight,
Music flows, enchanting night,
With every wave, a tale we weave,
In the depths, we dare believe.

Secrets of the Celestial Surf

Upon the crest of foamy waves,
Lies a magic that it saves,
Secrets spun like morning mist,
In the surf, a mystic tryst.

Stars reflect on watery glass,
In this realm, our worries pass,
Whispers of the cosmos bright,
In the depths, a dance of light.

Glistening shells, old and wise,
Guard the truths beneath the skies,
As the tides begin to rise,
Secrets bloom, a sweet surprise.

The ocean's heart beats strong and true,
With every swell, its stories brew,
Casting nets of dreams to share,
With the world, a wondrous fare.

In soft foam where wishes drift,
The celestial waves begin to lift,
Holding close the dreams that flow,
Secrets of the surf will glow.

Illuminated Ripples of Merfolk's Song

Beneath the waves, a chorus thrives,
With every ripple, magic dives,
Merfolk sing with voices pure,
Echoes of a lost allure.

In luminous depths, they weave their spells,
Hidden wonders, ocean dwells,
Chants that spark the waters' gleam,
Crafting twinkles, like a dream.

Silver fins in twilight dance,
To the rhythm of the sea's romance,
Their laughter drifts on gentle air,
Calling souls to come and share.

Twilight's hues and velvet nights,
Kiss the sea with stolen lights,
Beneath the surface, beauty lies,
In the heart of sonic sighs.

With each note, the currents flow,
Guiding dreams where few may go,
In this realm, so rich and free,
Ripples of song call out to me.

Prismatic Murmurs in the Aquatic Abyss

In the abyss, colors blend,
Murmurs rise, like ocean's friend,
Prismatic hues cast light anew,
Dancing shadows, deep and true.

Fathoms deep, where whispers call,
Beauty's echo, a silent thrall,
Glimmers of life in shadowed depths,
Swaying softly, nature's breaths.

With every murmur, stories spin,
Of shipwrecks lost and dreams within,
A tapestry of lore unfolds,
In aquatic hushed folds it holds.

From coral blooms to silky strands,
Mysteries thread through ancient lands,
Each prismatic wave, a song,
A celebration where hearts belong.

In the dark, where colors play,
Murmurs guide us on our way,
Within the depths, we find our peace,
As we drift, our souls release.

The Siren's Enigmatic Call

In twilight's hush, where whispers dwell,
A haunting song begins to swell.
With silvery notes that drift and weave,
It beckons those who dare believe.

The sailors pause, their hearts a-flutter,
As the sea sings softly, sweet as butter.
A tale of dreams entwined in brine,
Where fishers' fates in echoes twine.

Yet hidden sharp beneath the sound,
Lies a warning, dark and profound.
For beauty wraps a chilling fate,
As ships sail close to whispered bait.

Through moonlit waves, the sirens call,
In shadows deep, where echoes thrall.
To hear the song, one must be wise,
For what seems sweet can claim the skies.

So tread with care on ocean breeze,
For not all charms bring hearts at ease.
In every note, a choice lies bare,
Which path to take, a soul laid bare.

Melodies of Sun-kissed Shores

In golden light where waters dance,
The waves hum tunes of sweet romance.
With laughter bright, the children play,
As sunlit dreams drift far away.

The gulls, they sing, in joyful flight,
A chorus bright against twilight.
Each grain of sand holds stories old,
Of whispered secrets, brave and bold.

The ocean breeze, a soothing balm,
It wraps the world in soothing calm.
As tides embrace the moonlit night,
Each melody enchants the sight.

The horizon glows with colors true,
A canvas brushed in every hue.
Where sea and sky begin to meet,
The heart finds rhythms soft and sweet.

Within this realm, our spirits soar,
As nature sings, forevermore.
In sun-kissed shores, we find our way,
In every note, a bright bouquet.

Fantasies Crafted by the Sea

Upon the shore, the stories gleam,
Each ripple weaves a wondrous dream.
Where shells and whispers softly blend,
The sea's embrace knows no end.

With every wave, a tale unfolds,
Of ships that sailed with dreams of gold.
In coral reefs, bright treasures lie,
Where mermaids laugh and seagulls cry.

The salt-kissed air, a fragrant blend,
Brings forth the magic time can bend.
Beneath the stars, the ocean sighs,
As mysteries waltz in midnight skies.

Each twilight drapes the world in grace,
As tides reshape the ocean's face.
In every splash, a wish is cast,
A longing for a future vast.

With dreams that drift like clouds on high,
The sea sings gently a lullaby.
In hearts that listen, hope shall bloom,
From fantasies that chase the gloom.

Shadows of the Sea Sprite

In twilight's glow, where shadows creep,
A sprite awakes from ocean's sleep.
With silver hair and eyes like night,
She flits through foam, a fleeting sight.

Her laughter weaves through tangled weeds,
A melody that whispers deeds.
In moonlit paths, she dances free,
Her essence mingled with the sea.

The tides respond to her soft call,
As waves embrace the sea sprite's thrall.
With every leap, the waters gleam,
A flicker of her timeless dream.

Yet shadows loom where she may tread,
For darkness hints at paths once led.
In deep abyss, where secrets lay,
Lurks the unknown, always at play.

So heed the tales of long ago,
Of sprites and sea, of ebb and flow.
For in the depths of ocean's heart,
All wonder lives, a fragile art.

Gossamer Waves of Ethereal Light

In twilight's grace, the shadows dance,
Glimmers of magic, a fleeting glance.
Waves of silver softly rise,
Veils of dreams beneath the skies.

Whispers of twilight, secrets unfold,
Stories of starlight, cherished gold.
The moon's soft glow weaves through the night,
Illuminating paths of pure delight.

With each gentle crest, the night does sing,
Carving a tale, the heavens bring.
In every shimmer, in every ray,
Lies the hope of a brand new day.

Gossamer threads, like thoughts in flight,
Weaving together the dark and light.
Captured in moments, forever bright,
In the embrace of the endless night.

Lullabies from the Deep Blue

In the depths where silence reigns,
Beneath the waves, enchanting strains.
Echoes of lullabies sweetly flow,
Carried by currents, gentle and slow.

A melody born of star-kissed seas,
Softly whispers through the swaying trees.
Each note a promise, each chord a sigh,
Cradled in dreams, as the tides comply.

The ocean cradles a world so wide,
Creatures and wonders in soft abide.
As twilight dances on water's crest,
A lullaby beckons, inviting rest.

With every wave, the night unfolds,
Tales of adventure, secrets untold.
The stars above, like eyes so true,
Watch o'er the journey, the brave and few.

Reflections in a Sapphire Pool

Beneath the boughs, a sapphire gleams,
Mirrored beneath, the heart of dreams.
Ripples frame the secrets kept,
In water depths where whispers slept.

A world of wonders swirls and glows,
With every glance, the magic flows.
Dancing lights in the inky night,
Drawing all souls to their heart's delight.

In the stillness, visions weave,
Stories of what we wish to achieve.
Glimpses of futures, and echoes past,
Reflections in water, forever cast.

The sapphire pool holds tales untold,
Of dreams pursued, and hearts bold.
Every ripple a moment to save,
In the embrace of this tranquil wave.

Tidal Rhythms of Enchantment

The ocean's pulse beats soft and low,
In harmony with the moon's glow.
Tidal whispers echo through the land,
A song of magic, gentle and grand.

With every rise, a breath of light,
Each fall a promise, a soothing night.
In the dance of water, spirits play,
Guiding the night towards break of day.

Softly swaying, the world takes pause,
In nature's rhythm, we find our cause.
Tales of old wrapped in the tide,
Carved from the sands, where dreams abide.

Through frothy crests and twilight hues,
Nature sings of ancient views.
With every wave that rolls ashore,
The heart unfolds to seek for more.

Flourish of Diver's Enchanted Thoughts

Beneath the waves, where secrets lay,
A diver swims, in dreams astray.
Thoughts bloom like coral, bright and bold,
In sunlit depths, their tales unfold.

Mysteries dance in currents swift,
Each whispered wave, a sacred gift.
The ocean hums a ancient lore,
Inviting minds to seek and explore.

With every breath, the magic flows,
In twilight's glow, the wonder grows.
The heart attunes to nature's song,
Where time is short, but dreams aren't long.

Silence cradles the glowing light,
As starlit echoes pierce the night.
In every pulse of flowing sea,
Enchanted thoughts embrace the free.

The Magic of Tidepool Murmurs

In tidepools deep, where worlds collide,
Small wonders dwell, like dreams inside.
Each creature hides a tale to tell,
In pebbled beds, they weave their spell.

Whispers rise from the frothy shore,
A symphony of life to explore.
Starfish and shells, a vibrant array,
Invite the heart to pause and stay.

With gentle hands, the tides reveal,
The magic grasped in every feel.
A dance of light in the swirling foam,
In every nook, the sea finds home.

The breeze carries laughter, soft and sweet,
Where children's footsteps meet the beat.
In nature's arms, worries subside,
In tidepool realms, love will abide.

Submerged Fantasies in Celestial Waters

In depths of night, where dreams can swim,
The stars reflect on water's hymn.
Each ripple holds a wishful spark,
As fantasies glow in the endless dark.

Through azure depths, the spirits play,
Dancing gently, they guide the way.
To lands unknown where magic lies,
Beneath the swell of midnight skies.

A call of sirens, a haunting tone,
Invites us deeper, to realms unknown.
With every stroke, our worries cease,
In submerged fantasies, we find peace.

The moonlight bathes the ocean's face,
In shimmering dreams, we find our place.
Drifting further, the heart takes flight,
In celestial waters, love ignites.

Colors of the Ocean's Breath

The ocean hums in colors bright,
A symphony of day and night.
In swirling greens and azure blue,
Life dances forth, forever new.

From coral reefs to twilight's glow,
Each hue reveals a tale to sow.
Violet depths and golden sands,
A canvas born from nature's hands.

Rays filter down through water's embrace,
Painting dreams in a wavy trace.
The ocean's breath, a whisper sweet,
Where vibrant colors rise and meet.

With every wave, the stories fade,
Yet in our hearts, their echoes stayed.
In colors bright, we find our path,
In the ocean's breath, we learn to laugh.

Ethereal Softness in Gabrielle's Wave

In twilight's grip, the whispers flow,
A dance of light where dreamers go.
With breath of sea and scent of pine,
The waves enchant, your heart they twine.

Upon the shore, the silver sands,
Hold secrets shared by moonlit hands.
A gentle kiss, the tide's embrace,
Each moment felt, a timeless grace.

The lull of night, so soft, so sweet,
Where gorgeous shells and shadows meet.
Each feathered breeze, a soft refrain,
In Gabrielle's wave, love's quiet gain.

As starlit skies pour dreams like rain,
The ocean sings her softest strain.
With every crest, a story spun,
Ethereal touch, two souls in one.

Melody of an Ocean's Heartbeat

Beneath the waves, the secrets hum,
Where salt and sun weave life's sweet drum.
Each tide a pulse, a whispered song,
A melody where dreams belong.

The ocean's heart, vast and profound,
In every splash, a grace is found.
With every swell, the world stands still,
A harmony, the soul to fill.

From shore to depth, the echoes play,
Through rocky crags and golden bay.
A timeless waltz, the sea's own art,
In every wave, there beats a heart.

As seagulls cry, and sunsets gleam,
The water shimmers, the world a dream.
In every drift, a story twined,
The ocean's song, for hearts aligned.

An Aquatic Waltz of Sirens

In depths enchanted, sirens sing,
Their voices blend, a silken ring.
With braids of seaweed, flowing free,
They twirl and glide, near rocks and lea.

Emerald waters, kissed by light,
Their laughter dances through the night.
With twinkling eyes, and shimmering scales,
They weave through realms where beauty pales.

From coral thrones, they weave their charm,
With echoes bright to cast alarm.
But hearts ensnared, will always sway,
To sirens' calls, in moonlit play.

O tranquil waves, hold memories dear,
As twilight weaves the stars so near.
In each embrace, a magic born,
An aquatic waltz at break of dawn.

Ripples of Celestial Mirth

In cosmic tides, the stars align,
With every swirl, the light will shine.
Celestial dances craft the night,
In ripples soft, a pure delight.

The universe, a wondrous stream,
Reflects our hopes, our fleeting dream.
As galaxies spin and comets play,
In pools of starlight, we drift away.

With each soft wave, a laugh takes flight,
Beneath the heavens, glowing bright.
In every ripple, joy ignites,
A tapestry of endless nights.

Through cosmic seas, our spirits soar,
In laughter sweet, forevermore.
In every breath, the mirth cascades,
In ripples blessed, love never fades.

The Echoing Heartbeat of the Abyss

In shadows deep where silence creeps,
The heartbeat drifts, in darkness keeps.
Whispers of tales from ages past,
Echoes whisper, shadows cast.

A depth where light can scarcely tread,
Creatures dance with dreams unsaid.
Their lullabies weave through the night,
A symphony of lost delight.

With every pulse, a secret spun,
The abyss sighs, its journey begun.
Tides of time in restless flow,
Unraveling things we long to know.

Beneath the waves, a lantern glows,
Guiding hearts where no one goes.
In vast and boundless, haunting seas,
The echoing drum of mysteries.

So listen close, let silence speak,
In every beat, the lost will seek.
Pooling shadows, dreams in thrall,
The heartbeat whispers through it all.

Dances of the Ethereal Currents

Where spirits sway in currents light,
They spin and twirl, a magical sight.
With ghostly grace, they glide and sweep,
In watery realms where secrets keep.

The tides compose a waltz divine,
As moonlit beams and shadows twine.
Each flicker tells a tale untold,
In hues of azure, silver, gold.

A gentle push, a playful tease,
Through currents strong, they glide with ease.
Beneath the waves, a dance unfolds,
In whispered breaths, the ocean holds.

With every arc of flippered grace,
The dance enchants this hidden place.
Swirls and sways, a fluid art,
In every motion, beats the heart.

As stars above begin to gleam,
The currents blend with a sailor's dream.
Where water meets the sky's embrace,
The ethereal dance finds its place.

Serenade of the Forgotten Depths

In faded depths where silence sleeps,
The serenade of past time seeps.
Through ancient stones with stories lost,
A melody drifts, no matter the cost.

Forgotten voices call in the hush,
With every rise, a haunting rush.
In spiraled shells and crumbled reefs,
They sing of sorrow, joy, and grief.

Ripples carry their tender sighs,
As currents weave through dreaming skies.
A lullaby of shadows low,
In the embrace of ebb and flow.

Beneath the waves, the echoes blend,
The serenade, an ocean's friend.
In whispered tones, the depths will share,
The essence of those lost in despair.

So linger long where memories wade,
Listen close to the serenade.
In depths unknown, the heart will find,
A music sweet, yet undefined.

A Symphony of Aquatic Hues

In vibrant swirls of azure light,
An symphony bursts in colors bright.
The sea's embrace, a canvas wide,
Where every wave has lived and died.

Pinks and greens in harmony hum,
Beneath the waves, a grandiose drum.
Tangled kelp and whispers flow,
In vibrant notes of undertow.

A chorus sings to coral groves,
In strains of wonder, nature roves.
The ocean's heart, a melody bold,
In every hue, a story told.

The sunlit dance on liquid glass,
Creates new symphonies as they pass.
With tides that rise and fall in tune,
The aquatic hues beneath the moon.

Listen closely, let your heart be free,
The ocean's symphony, wild and free.
In every splash, a timeless clue,
The symphony of aquatic hues.

Whimsical Gleams of Seafoam Dreams

In the hush of the moon's soft glow,
Whispers dance where the secrets flow.
Mermaids laugh in a crystal stream,
Binding tales in a magical dream.

Waves weave wonders, a shimmering hue,
Glimmers of hope in the ocean's blue.
Stars cast reflections, both bold and bright,
Painting the depths with enchanting light.

Shells sing songs on the sandy shore,
Each a story, a myth to explore.
Ebbing and flowing, the tides take flight,
Carrying visions through the gentle night.

Bubbles of laughter, a frothy delight,
Swaying to rhythms of the sea's heartbeat.
In every crest, a promise is born,
Of journeys anew with each breaking dawn.

Beneath the surface, magic unfolds,
In the whispers of tides, adventure holds.
So let your spirit drift and roam free,
In this world of enchantment, come dream with me.

Chants of the Submerged Stardust

In the depths where the shadows play,
Echoes of starlight softly sway.
Barnacles cradle the stories of yore,
While ancient whispers through waters soar.

Coral kingdoms, a vivid embrace,
Guarding the secrets of time and space.
Aquatic ballads, an ethereal sound,
Resonate gently where wonders abound.

From seaweed forests to deep ocean glades,
Mysteries lurk in the shimmering shades.
Fish clad in colors both strange and rare,
Dance in the currents, light as the air.

Drifting on tides of a silky night,
The moon's silver fingers weave dreams in flight.
Each swell and surge a melodic refrain,
Woven from stardust, a mystical chain.

Lost in the beauty of sparkling streams,
The ocean sings softly of shimmering dreams.
Follow the music, let it guide you near,
To the essence of magic, forever clear.

Luminous Threads of Tide's Embrace

Under the cloak of a twilight haze,
Lies the whisper of night in a silvery phase.
Stars in their splendor stitch shadows of light,
Weaving the darkness, enchanting the night.

Ripples of laughter curl in the air,
Flickering hopes on the ocean's fair.
Tidal caresses, a gentle hold,
Stories of love in each wave retold.

In shimmering patterns, the currents unfurl,
Guiding lost dreams in a luminous whirl.
Seashells cast glimmers, like wishes set free,
A tapestry rich with the pulse of the sea.

With each ebbing tide, a soft serenade,
Echoes of joy in the twilight parade.
The world seems to pause in this magical trance,
Held in the arms of the sea's sweet dance.

So gather your dreams, let them rise and flow,
In the luminous threads of the tide's warm glow.
For here in the depths of the ocean's spawn,
Lies the heart of a story, forever drawn.

Enchanted Harmonies of Coral and Shell

In a realm where the coral blooms bright,
Gentle creatures sway in soft, filtered light.
The ocean hums hymns of joy and delight,
Orchestrating waves in a dance of the night.

A symphony woven with each golden ray,
Nature's own music that guides the way.
Seahorses twirl in a whimsical waltz,
Embracing the magic where time comes to halt.

Echoes of laughter from fish schools below,
Chorusing softly as currents bestow.
Their melodies twine with the gentle sea breeze,
Composing a tapestry meant to appease.

Dancing along with the ebb and the flow,
Shells whisper secrets that only they know.
Each grain of sand, a note in the score,
Melodies linger forever on shore.

Lets hearts be lifted by sweet ocean calls,
As nature enchants with her lyrical thralls.
In this haven of dreams, we find our peace,
Where harmony reigns and all worries cease.

Hymns of the Moonlit Waters

In silver beams the river flows,
Awakening the night's soft prose.
Whispers dance on gentle waves,
While shadows sigh in twilight's graves.

Stars above like lanterns gleam,
As secrets weave through silver seam.
Each ripple sings a tale of old,
Of lovers' dreams and hearts of gold.

An owl calls from the woodland deep,
Guarding stories that we keep.
Moonlit paths that wander far,
Lead us to where wonders are.

The nightingale sings her sweet lull,
In harmony with the waters' pull.
Crickets chirp their nightly rhyme,
As the world slips into time.

So let us stroll by the liquid light,
Where dreams take flight in silky night.
For in the heart of nature's grace,
We find our home, our sacred place.

Treasures in Twilight's Cascade

Beneath the hush of fading day,
A tapestry of dreams will play.
Upon the rocks, the waters gleam,
Reflecting hopes, like stars, they beam.

With every drop that meets the stone,
A story whispered, softly grown.
The twilight paints with colors rare,
Illuminating secrets laid bare.

Hidden gems in cascading streams,
Hold promises wrapped in moonlit dreams.
Nature's gift, a precious find,
With every wave, the heart entwined.

As shadows stretch and day departs,
The river carries all our hearts.
In twilight's glow, we let them soar,
To places vast, to distant shores.

So gather 'round, let stories flow,
In twilight's dance, let feelings grow.
For treasures here will never fade,
In the cascade where dreams are made.

Lullabies of the Ocean's Breath

The ocean hums a soothing tune,
Beneath the watchful silver moon.
Each wave a whisper, soft and light,
A lullaby that steals the night.

With every crash upon the shore,
The sea reveals its ancient lore.
The currents swirl like gentle hands,
Embracing dreams from distant lands.

Mermaids weave in foamy trails,
While starlit boats tell wondrous tales.
A breeze that kisses salty air,
Carries secrets for those who dare.

The lullabies of tides will sway,
And cradle hearts in sweet decay.
So let the ocean's whispers guide,
As we, like shells, in peace abide.

For in the breath of endless waves,
We find the solace that love craves.
A song of life, of joy, of jest,
On ocean's breath, we find our rest.

Echoed Dreams Beneath the Surf

In the depths where shadows play,
Echoed dreams of yesterday.
The ocean holds the whispers close,
Of hope and fear, of love engrossed.

Beneath the foam, a world awakes,
With every rise, and fall, it shakes.
A symphony of tides and time,
Where every note feels like a rhyme.

Through coral halls, and sunlit beams,
Lies the heart of all our dreams.
Each echo from the ocean's heart,
Reminds us all we share a part.

So dive into this deep abyss,
For treasure lies in every kiss.
The tides will bring us back to shore,
Where echoes dance forevermore.

In surf's embrace, we find our way,
Among the whispers, night and day.
For in the sea's eternal song,
We learn where we truly belong.

The Dance of Underwater Shadows

In depths where sunlight fades, they glide,
Whispers of the sea, in secrecy, abide.
Shadows twist and turn, in a waltz so grand,
They tell of tales lost, from a long-lost land.

With currents swirling soft, they play their tune,
A symphony of silence, beneath the moon.
Each scale a note, each fin a sigh,
Echoes of magic where time drifts by.

Colors merge in hues, like dreams unfurled,
Beneath the waves, a hidden world.
Corals weave stories on ancient stones,
In the heart of the ocean, their beauty moans.

The dance weaves on, as twilight nears,
Murmurs of the past, lost in the years.
Together they echo, in the inky deep,
Secrets of the sea, in shadows they keep.

Lush Currents of Distant Echoes

Beyond the waves, in twilight's glow,
Currents of dreams in the deep below.
They beckon with whispers of things unseen,
Stories of places where the sky is green.

With each plunge and rise, the heart will flutter,
In gardens of kelp where the soft waves shudder.
Seaweed dances, in rhythms profound,
Echoes of laughter beneath the sound.

Fishes flash like stars, in a veil of night,
Guiding lost souls with their flickering light.
In the watery ballet, they swirl and sway,
Carrying secrets of the ocean's play.

Through swirls of brine, history unfurls,
Legends of mermaids, and treasure in pearls.
Ancient cities rest, in slumbering peace,
In lush currents, time finds its release.

Harmonies of Lost Treasures

In caverns deep, where sunlight wanes,
Lies the melody of forgotten chains.
Harmonies rise from the ocean floor,
Chanting the tales of love and more.

Gold coins rustle in a shimmering sea,
Echoes of laughter, wild and free.
Siren songs call to the hearts of the brave,
To seek out treasures their spirits crave.

With shells as instruments, the tides compose,
Notes of adventure in the ebb and flows.
Mysterious whispers weave through the waves,
A ballad of sailors, lost in their graves.

Each shimmer and glint, a story untold,
In harmonies hid, that never grow old.
To dive is to dance, in a world full of dreams,
Where nothing is ever quite what it seems.

Beneath the Silver Veil of Dusk

As day yields softly to the night's embrace,
The ocean is cloaked in silver lace.
Beneath the stars, where dreams take flight,
Mysteries awaken in the velvety light.

The tide hums low, a lullaby sweet,
Cradling the shores in a rhythmic beat.
Moonlight glitters like diamonds on waves,
Painting reflections where enchantment saves.

In stillness, the deep holds stories untold,
Of ships that sailed and the sailors bold.
Lost in the currents, they wander and roam,
In the heart of the ocean, they find their home.

With whispers of night, the sea breathes slow,
Carrying secrets, in currents that flow.
Beneath the silver veil, where shadows play,
Legends awaken at the end of the day.

Whispers of the Ocean Serenade

Upon the waves, a gentle sigh,
The sea hums softly, asking why.
With every crest, a tale unfolds,
Of ancient ships and treasures bold.

Beneath the stars, the moonlight gleams,
In watery depths, where mystery dreams.
The ocean's breath—soft secrets weave,
In lullabies that hearts believe.

Fishermen's songs in twilight's glow,
Whisper of currents, ebbing slow.
Each splash a memory, long since told,
In rhythms of blue, and stories of old.

The tide pulls tight, the night enthralls,
The ceaseless dance, as silence calls.
With every wave that's kissed by time,
A serenade of salt and rhyme.

So listen close, to ocean's tune,
Under the watchful, silver moon.
In every whisper, find a home,
In depths of dreams where souls may roam.

Secrets Beneath the Coral Mirror

In sunlit realms where colors blaze,
Coral gardens in a blissful haze.
The sea's embrace holds secrets true,
Whispers of magic in vibrant hue.

Anemones dance, a current's sway,
As shadows flicker at close of day.
Fish dart swiftly, a jeweled parade,
In a kingdom where dreams are made.

Hidden treasures, each crevice hides,
Stories of ages, where mystery bides.
With every ripple, an echo calls,
From the heart of the ocean, the deepest halls.

Beneath the surface, magic brews,
In mirrored depths of emerald blues.
Life intertwines in graceful art,
An ocean's soul, where wonders start.

So dive within, where secrets dwell,
In coral realms, weaves a spell.
Awake the stories, let them unfurl,
In oceanic dreams, embark and swirl.

Echoes of a Breaching Dream

A breach of light, a splash of night,
The ocean speaks in sheer delight.
A dance in blue, a leap of grace,
Whales sing softly, a timeless trace.

In surf and spray, the world holds breath,
Each surge of wave whispers of death.
Yet life persists beneath the foam,
In ocean's heart, all creatures roam.

Glistening with stories, deep and wide,
Echoes resound where spirits glide.
The song of the sea is bittersweet,
A melody beneath the beat.

Drifting clouds above, an endless dream,
Reflections dance, shimmer, and gleam.
Every splash a secret shared,
In echoes of love, none unprepared.

So close your eyes, hear the call,
The ocean's pulse, the rise and fall.
In dreaming tides, find solace near,
In each crashing wave, feel no fear.

Celestial Siren's Lament

In moonlit tides, where shadows sway,
A siren's song pulls hearts away.
Her voice, a caress of night's embrace,
Yearning for souls in a timeless chase.

Upon the rocks, the waters sigh,
Secrets of love and longing high.
With every note, the stars align,
In heavenly chords, where fates entwine.

The ocean weeps, her silent plea,
For lovers lost in the boundless sea.
Each wave a whisper, soft and low,
In depths of sorrow, a tender flow.

Yet hope resides in the heart's refrain,
A light in the dark, through joy and pain.
In siren's lament, a truth shines bright,
That love endures beyond the night.

So hear her call in the misty air,
A melody spun with haunting care.
With every drop, the ocean sighs,
In celestial dreams, where love never dies.

Whispers Beneath the Ocean's Veil

Beneath the waves, a tale untold,
Where mysteries of the deep unfold.
In shadows paint, a world so bright,
The ocean's sighs ignite the night.

Whispers dance on currents strong,
In every tide, a secret song.
With silver scales and fins that gleam,
The ocean weaves a timeless dream.

Crashing foam and crashing hearts,
As nature's beauty plays its parts.
The dolphins leap, the starlight fades,
In watery realms where magic wades.

Moonlit paths on the ocean's face,
Guide lost souls to a warm embrace.
Together we chase the shimmering dew,
Where the sea cradles dreams anew.

The siren's song, a luring call,
Beckons the brave, ensnares them all.
Eternity spins in each gentle swell,
In the depths where enchantments dwell.

Melodies from the Deep Blue

In the heart of the ocean's song,
Melodies weave where souls belong.
With every wave, a note takes flight,
The deep blue hums in the still night.

Coral blooms and creatures play,
In rhythm with night, in dance with day.
Each splash and ripple holds a tune,
A chorus sung beneath the moon.

Echoes of laughter, whispers of fears,
The ocean shares both joys and tears.
Through tides that rise and tides that fall,
The deep resounds with nature's call.

Shimmering fishes chase the light,
In a ballet of color, pure delight.
The current spins a wondrous thread,
Binding stories of the living and dead.

O, sing with me, ye sea and sky,
In harmony, let wonders fly.
For in this realm so vast and free,
Lies the heart of eternity.

Secrets of the Siren's Lullaby

In twilight's hush, the waves obey,
As sirens weave their soft ballet.
With tender notes that swell and fall,
They beckon sailors, one and all.

The lullaby sings of dreams so rare,
A melody wrapped in salty air.
Secrets swirl in the ocean's hold,
Whispers of love and tales of old.

Glimmers of silver on the crest,
Where longing hearts find their rest.
With each sigh of the ocean's breath,
The sirens chant of life and death.

In moonlit waters, shadows glide,
Where beauty and danger coincide.
The rocks conceal, the depths combine,
In haunting tunes, their voices entwine.

So linger near, oh sailor bold,
Let stories of the sea unfold.
For every note born from the sea,
Holds the secret of you and me.

Echoes of the Wave-Kissed Shore

On shores where sea and land connect,
The waves bring tales we can't neglect.
With every crash, a memory wakes,
While salt and sand form gentle lakes.

Echoes of laughter kiss the night,
In every swirl, a spark ignites.
The shorelines whisper, soft and clear,
Of love stories etched through the years.

Seagulls call to the shimmering sea,
In search of treasures wild and free.
As shells lie scattered, secrets hide,
In rhythm with the ebbing tide.

Footprints linger, washed away,
But the heart remembers yesterday.
As oceans breathe, and time stands still,
The echoes linger, sweet and shrill.

So listen close, dear heart, take heed,
The ocean knows what souls need.
In wave-kissed dreams, let wanderlust soar,
For life's a journey to explore.

Subaqueous Glimpses of Desire

In the depths where secrets creep,
Shadows wander, softly seep.
Whispers murmur through the tide,
Yearnings that the heart can hide.

Fish like dreams, darting fast,
Flickers of what might then last.
Corals bloom in varied hues,
Echoing the soul's deep muse.

Moonlight dances on the floor,
Guiding souls to seek for more.
With each ripple, hearts align,
In the ocean's vast design.

Bubbles rise, hopes set free,
Floating on a gentle sea.
A treasure found, a fleeting glance,
In this world, we dare to dance.

Dreams submerged in aqueous lanes,
Holding fragile, sweet remains.
Submerge yourself, take a chance,
In the depths, let desires prance.

Ribbons of Reflected Light

Threads of gold and silver spun,
Chasing shadows, making fun.
Illuminating darkened nights,
Painting dreams in vibrant sights.

Every glimmer tells a tale,
Of lost loves and winds that wail.
Within the ripples, stories weave,
In the light, we learn to believe.

Glistening paths where hopes can soar,
A dance upon the ocean's floor.
Each twinkling star a guiding spark,
Leading souls from dusk to dark.

Amidst the waves, a laughter sings,
Echoing the joy it brings.
Captured moments, time's delight,
In the ribbons of reflected light.

And as the sun begins to set,
Dreams are sewn with no regret.
In every hue, in every shade,
The magic of the night is laid.

Melancholy of the Beneath

Deep below where silence dwells,
A heartache only darkness tells.
Echoes of a once-bright flame,
Carried softly, void of name.

Whispers linger in the dark,
Yearning for a hidden spark.
Beneath the waves, the shadows sigh,
As lost dreams float and gently die.

The weight of water holds me down,
Chained to sorrow's haunting crown.
In the depths, where sorrows rest,
Lies a longing, unexpressed.

Salted tears, the ocean's taste,
All the chances laid to waste.
In the stillness, silence swells,
A haunting song, the ocean's knells.

Yet in that mournful space, I find,
Fragments of hope intertwined.
A spark beneath the tranquil sea,
Awakens all that was meant to be.

Dance of the Buoyant Stars

Floating light in endless night,
Stars twirl and spin, a wondrous sight.
With each beat of cosmic grace,
They beckon dreams to join the chase.

A galaxy of wishes bright,
Whispers carried on the light.
Celestial bodies sway and glide,
Inviting hearts to turn the tide.

In the vastness, joy takes flight,
As galaxies ignite the night.
In this cosmic waltz, we tread,
Chasing visions yet unsaid.

Stars entwined in a radiant show,
Gliding paths only stardust knows.
Each twinkling pulse a story spun,
In the dance, we become as one.

So close your eyes and dream anew,
Amidst the stars, pure magic's hue.
In this ballet, fears soon depart,
For in each dance, there beats a heart.

The Celestial Choir of the Sea

In the cool embrace of silken tides,
Voices rise where the ocean hides,
Melodies woven with salt and light,
As stars above gleam through the night.

Each wave a note in harmony's song,
A rhythm of longing that carries us along,
Shells whisper secrets of ages gone by,
A timeless symphony beneath the sky.

The moonlight dances on water's crest,
Inviting all dreamers to seek their rest,
With lullabies sung in the ocean's breath,
A magical realm full of life and death.

In the distance, a siren's call,
Echoes enchanting, a sweet enthrall,
From depths where the sunbeams barely reach,
An ode to the heart that the sea can teach.

So listen closely, let the waves explain,
The stories of joy and the tales of pain,
For in each swell and crash of foam,
The celestial choir has found its home.

Hidden Choirs in the Tidal Dance

Beneath the surface, where shadows play,
Hidden choirs weave through night and day,
In currents soft and undercurrents bold,
Ancient songs of the deep unfold.

Glimmers of light flicker from afar,
Upon the stage where the sea creatures are,
Each ripple carries a note unseen,
A tapestry stitched in silver and green.

When storms arise and the waters roar,
The choir grows fierce, a wild encore,
Blending fury with grace in a far-off trance,
Nature's voice in a tempestuous dance.

As tides recede, the whispers float,
Serene sonatas on a driftwood boat,
And all who listen may find their hearts,
Bound to the ocean where magic starts.

In the twilight hours, the songs reveal,
Secrets of treasures the waves conceal,
With every swell, a promise renews,
The hidden choirs forever infused.

Wistful Whispers of the Briny Depths

In the briny depths where shadows dwell,
Wistful whispers weave a lasting spell,
Softly spoken in the water's embrace,
Tales of the past drift in endless grace.

Coral castles hold memories dear,
Echoes of laughter, the joy, and the fear,
Each crack and crevice a canvas for time,
Where stories are etched, a rhythm and rhyme.

The currents murmur of journeys long,
Adventures taken, both right and wrong,
With every undertow, a pull to the past,
Wistful reminders that love cannot last.

Creatures murmur in softest tones,
Their ancient wisdom like whispered groans,
For those who seek, the depths reveal,
A song of sorrow, a heart to heal.

So let the tides wash over your soul,
Embrace the echoes, let them make you whole,
For in the sea's breath, life finds a way,
Wistful whispers of night and day.

Melancholy Reflections in Aquamarine Shimmers

In the aquamarine, reflections gleam,
Melancholy dances on the surface, it seems,
A palette of feelings in swirling light,
Where daydreams linger and fade from sight.

The horizon blushes with pastel hues,
As thoughts drift away like scattered clues,
Each ripple holds a lost memory's gaze,
A fleeting glimpse of the past's soft blaze.

Beneath the waves, where shadows meet,
The world sighs in a sweet retreat,
Melancholic whispers of hope and despair,
In the cradle of waves, they wander and share.

A lull of the ocean, a heart's quiet plea,
Reminding us all of the depths of the sea,
Each swell brings forth a sorrowful tune,
A hymn to the night and the silvered moon.

So gaze into the depths, embrace what you see,
The melancholy reflections that shape you and me,
For in every shimmer, a story unfurls,
Melancholy echoes of our intertwined worlds.

A Song for the Drowning Stars

In the velvet quilt of night,
Stars whisper secrets, softly bright,
Each twinkle a tale of ancient light,
Falling quickly, lost from sight.

Beneath the waves of time they sink,
Silent echoes, hearts that think,
A serenade of dreams, they link,
To the depths where shadows blink.

Tides that pull both high and low,
Carry whispers, full of woe,
Yet in their sway, the night will glow,
With stories only starlight knows.

When dawn emerges, they fade away,
Yet linger in the break of day,
A sigh upon the waves' ballet,
In memory, they boldly stay.

So sing to stars that fall from grace,
A melody in empty space,
For in their loss, we find our place,
A song of love we shall embrace.

Serpentine Glide Through Salty Skies

Waves crest gently, winds do sigh,
Above the seas where gulls do fly,
Through salty air, their shadows lie,
In nature's dance, we roam and sigh.

Beneath the clouds, the ocean swirls,
In depths unknown, the mystery unfurls,
A serpentine glide where the horizon twirls,
Silent whispers, soft as pearls.

Riding currents, wild and free,
The seaweed sways, a graceful plea,
A ballet on waves, just you and me,
In liquid dreams, we yearn to be.

With every crest, our hearts will soar,
Together we glide, forever explore,
Through salty skies and skies of yore,
In nature's arms, we can't ignore.

So let us chase the fading light,
As day turns softly into night,
With every breath, our spirits ignite,
In serpentines of pure delight.

Fragments of a Lost Oceanic Tale

In the whirlpool's grasp, a story waits,
Of ships long gone and ancient fates,
With every wave, the past elates,
Fragmented dreams on the ocean's plates.

Ghostly echoes of sailors' calls,
Haunting whispers as twilight falls,
Tales drift gently on water's walls,
In the shadow where silence sprawls.

Shells and stones hold time's embrace,
Each grain of sand a fleeting trace,
Of laughter lost in the ocean's grace,
In fragments of this hidden place.

Resonating with the moon's soft glow,
The sea reveals what we should know,
Fragments of light in ebb and flow,
A tale of love, forever low.

So gather 'round, let history sail,
In whispered waves, the olden trail,
For in the depths, the voices hale,
Fragments weave the timeless tale.

The Enigma of Moonlit Waters

Beneath the moon's enchanting gaze,
The water dances, lost in a haze,
Ripples whisper in soft arrays,
An enigma wrapped in silver blaze.

Secrets linger where shadows play,
In the heart of night, dreams stray,
A gentle call from far away,
Where ocean's song leads souls to stay.

Stars reflect in a tranquil tide,
Guiding hearts, our fears subside,
In the stillness, we'd confide,
The soothing balm of the moonlit ride.

With every wave, a story flows,
A thousand years in ebbs and throes,
The waters hold what nobody knows,
In the dance of night, the secret glows.

So come, my friend, let us embark,
To chase the dreams where whispers hark,
For in the depths, we'll leave our mark,
In moonlit waters, we'll find the spark.

The Allure of Shimmering Shadows

In twilight's gentle, golden gleam,
Where whispers dance upon a dream,
The shadows shimmer, secrets spill,
A dance of magic, soft and still.

Among the trees, with bated breath,
The echoes speak of life and death,
Each flicker tells a tale untold,
Of hidden wonders, bright and bold.

The moonlight weaves a silken thread,
Binding the longing hearts, half-dead,
In shadows deep, where thoughts can roam,
The night's embrace becomes a home.

Each glimmer shares a world apart,
A whispered pulse within the heart,
And as the skies wear silver crowns,
The allure calls, the silence drowns.

So wander close, and take a chance,
Embrace the twilight's mystic dance,
For in the shadows, lives the light,
A truth obscured, yet shining bright.

A Tale of the Drowned Sea Fable

Once deep below the ocean's weep,
Where ancient secrets silently sleep,
A tale begins of those long lost,
Of treasures gained, and love's great cost.

The mermaids sing in sapphire waves,
Of sailors' dreams and watery graves,
Each note a promise, soft and sweet,
As currents weave in rhythmic beat.

Beneath the swell, where shadows play,
In currents dark, the echoes sway,
Their laughter mingles with despair,
A fable whispered on the air.

For pearls are cast through veils of time,
Entangled in the sea's sweet rhyme,
And lost are souls, but not in vain,
Their stories twist like ocean's chain.

So listen close, ye hearts awake,
To ocean's hymn, and waves that break,
For in the depths, the past be told,
In every shimmer, every fold.

Secrets of the Ebbing Twilight

As daylight wanes and shadows creep,
The world unfolds its secrets deep,
In twilight's arms, the quiet sighs,
A tapestry of whispered lies.

The stars emerge from velvet skies,
A constellation of goodbyes,
Each shimmering point a dream once bright,
Now tucked away in folds of night.

The breeze carries tales of old,
In voices soft, with echoes bold,
When dusk unveils its hidden truth,
A dance of time, a waltz of youth.

Amongst the leaves, a rustling sound,
As secrets pulse beneath the ground,
The ebbing twilight, a gentle thief,
Stealing whispers, granting grief.

So walk with care, ye seeker brave,
For twilight holds what few can save,
A world where dreams and shadows meet,
In every corner, wild and sweet.

The Melodic Fabric of the Sea

In ocean's heart, a symphony,
Waves dance and twine, wild and free,
Each note a splash, a call to play,
The fabric woven night and day.

The gulls take flight on whispers light,
While dolphins leap, their joy in sight,
The rhythm pulses, deep and bold,
A story longing to be told.

With every tide, a song is spun,
Of ancient tales, of battles won,
And lullabies from distant shores,
Carried on currents, forever explores.

The salted air, a gentle tease,
As melodies weave through the trees,
A harmony of land and sea,
A link between what's you and me.

So let the sea's sweet song resound,
In every heart, be joy profound,
For life's a wave, we ride and sway,
In the melodic fabric of the day.

Purring Whispers Beyond the Waves

When night enfolds the restless shore,
The purring whispers softly soar.
Above the tide's caressing sweep,
Secrets of the ocean deep.

A breeze adorned with tales untold,
Wraps the moon in silver cold.
Each ripple stirs a memory,
Of spirits dancing wild and free.

Cloaked in mist, a ship draws near,
Carrying songs of joy and fear.
The stars align in cosmic play,
Guiding dreams that drift away.

Beneath the glare of lantern light,
Fables fold into the night.
Voices drift like feathered kites,
Suspended in the heart of sights.

Yet in the depths where shadows dwell,
Whispers weave a wondrous spell.
For every wave that breaks ashore,
Holds echoes of the evermore.

Laces of Blued Dreams

In twilight's grasp where shadows blend,
Laces of dreams begin to mend.
Soft hues of blue that softly twine,
Woven threads of fate divine.

The murmurs of a distant flight,
Call forth the stars, ignite the night.
Each fleeting glimpse, a promise made,
In silken strands that never fade.

Cascading hopes in gentle spirals,
We dance to tunes of ancient tiles.
Through whispering winds and starlit hues,
The world blooms forth in blued reviews.

With every step, enchantments stir,
Waking echoes that were once now blurred.
The pathways fabled, trails anew,
Unravel mysteries once askew.

In moonlit dreams, the heart takes flight,
Where wishes weave, a pure delight.
Entwined in fate, forever bound,
In laces of dreams, love is found.

Oceanic Pirouette in Moonbeam

The ocean dances, an endless swirl,
In moonlit pirouettes that twirl.
Waves cascade in silver light,
An aquatic ballet through the night.

Stars reflect on the velvet sea,
Their twinkling steps in harmony.
With every crest a whisper flows,
Carrying secrets that ebb and pose.

A wayward breeze, a gentle tease,
Sways the heart like swaying trees.
The tides align in perfect grace,
Creating beauty as they embrace.

Frothy foams like delicate lace,
Paint stories in this sacred space.
Footprints washed in fleeting time,
Etched in memory, soft as chime.

In harmonious loops, rhythms sigh,
Where moonbeams find their lullaby.
As the ocean pirouettes and spins,
Hope refreshes, anew, it begins.

Enigmatic Swirls of Distant Echoes

Beyond the hills where shadows play,
Enigmatic echoes softly sway.
In spirals lost from time and place,
Whispers weave through empty space.

Fragments float on twilight's stream,
As stars emerge from folds of dream.
Every note a fading call,
Where silence stirs and shadows fall.

In corridors of ancient lore,
Footsteps trace what came before.
A melody of cryptic sighs,
Calls forth the truth beneath the lies.

Tales of wonder and of woe,
Spirited realms where few may go.
Voices linger on the breeze,
Embracing hearts with timeless ease.

Each echo blooms like flowers rare,
In twilight's breath, they swirl and share.
Through tangled paths, light starts to climb,
In enigmatic swirls, we find our rhyme.

Chime of the Enchanted Shell

In tides that weave the tales of old,
A shell lies whispering, secrets untold.
It sings of mermaids and waves that dance,
Of starlit nights and waves' romance.

With each soft chime, the echoes swell,
Of shipwrecked hearts and magic spell.
The ocean's breath, a lullaby sweet,
Guides lost souls to the surf's heartbeat.

In the moon's embrace, shadows take flight,
Carving stories in the shimmering light.
The enchanted shell calls, a siren's plea,
Unraveling wonders beneath the sea.

Listen closely, let your heart drift,
For in its depths, a precious gift.
The chime that hums of love's sweet quest,
Awakens dreams, and sets them to rest.

Ripples of Forgotten Legends

Beneath the waves, where shadows sleep,
Forgotten tales in silence creep.
Ripples ripple through time and space,
Carrying echoes of each brave face.

Once they tread on shores of gold,
Now in whispers, their stories unfold.
The sea embraces their fleeting breath,
In the dance of life, and the silence of death.

Legends linger in briny curls,
Where shells are jewels and hope unfurls.
Each wave that breaks, each tide that sways,
Holds the heart of lost summers' days.

Listen well, for the waters sing,
Of harbors safe and the joy they bring.
In each small ripple, a history lies,
Waiting for dreamers beneath the skies.

Secrets Cradled in Algae

In emerald depths, where mysteries bloom,
Algae cradle secrets in their green loom.
Silent guardians of whispers untold,
Beneath their veil, ancient stories unfold.

Beneath the tide, the world sways slow,
Each tendril a path where few dare go.
The old and the wise in the currents confide,
Where the shadows and light continually bide.

With each gentle wave, new tales arrive,
In tangled greens, the lost dreams thrive.
The ocean remembers what we often forget,
In the embrace of algae, our paths are set.

Let your heart wander to depths unforeseen,
Where magic and mystery quietly glean.
For in these waters, where the secrets lie,
The spirit of adventure will never say die.

Whispered Dreams in Aquamarine

In aquamarine, the world transforms,
Where daydreams dance and reality warms.
Bubbles rise, bearing wishes divine,
Whispered secrets in currents entwine.

The sun casts jewels on the surface bright,
Emerging visions in glowing light.
Secrets unfurl like sails in the breeze,
Carried by currents, with such gentle ease.

In stillness, dreams begin to roam,
Wandering far from their earthly home.
The spirit of water, wild and free,
Invites our hearts to wander the sea.

With every ripple, a tale of grace,
Echoes of laughter in this serene place.
So close your eyes and drift away,
In the realm of dreams, forever stay.

Haunting Secrets Nested in Kelp

In the depths of the kelp, shadows lie,
Where whispers of mysteries softly sigh.
With tendrils entwined in the fading light,
The ocean reveals secrets cloaked in night.

Ghostly echoes of stories untold,
In the silence of waters, the past unfolds.
Beneath the green sways, old ships rest now,
Guarded by creatures who once took a bow.

The moon casts its gaze on the murky ground,
Where lost treasures of sailors are finally found.
Harbors of memories, both grim and sweet,
Because time ebbs away, but memories repeat.

Tales of the brave who dared to roam,
In the heart of the depths, they found a home.
For every kelp forest, a history breathes,
As long as the tide, a soul never leaves.

In the dance of the waves, shadows retreat,
The haunting secrets, a bittersweet treat.
With each gentle rustle, the secrets awake,
In the vibrant embrace of the kelp's sweet ache.

The Pantomime of the Marine Beyond

Beneath the surface, life takes its stage,
With creatures of wonder who script their own page.
A ballet of fins in the shimmering sea,
The pantomime dances, wild and free.

Corals a-glimmer, with colors so bright,
As fish flit like laughter in morning light.
A sardine, a star, in this oceanic play,
Twists and turns in a joyous array.

The diver descends, a kind audience near,
Wonders of nature, alive with sheer cheer.
A sea anemone waves, a curtain call,
While turtles glide gracefully, capturing all.

Kelp forests sway to the rhythm so real,
An orchestra plays where the currents reveal.
In tune with the tides, the ocean's sweet song,
Its heart is a stage where all creatures belong.

As bubbles rise gently, the stories unfold,
Of life in the depths, both timid and bold.
In the pantomime's glow, we see what we seek:
The magic of marine is a language unique.

Mischief of Silvery Flickers

In the moonlit waters, the sprites take a dive,
With silvery flickers, they dance and arrive.
Glimmers of laughter in the wake of the tide,
Mischief afoot as the currents collide.

The fish dart and play in a dazzling array,
Silver scales glinting beneath the moon's ray.
They weave through the shadows, a playful embrace,
Chasing each other in a wild, timeless race.

Jellyfish float like the whispers of night,
Casting shadows that shimmer in ethereal light.
They swirl to a rhythm unknown to the keen,
In the heart of the sea, where mischief is seen.

A flick of a tail, the bubbles erupt,
As sprites quickly scatter, their secrets disrupt.
Every ripple and splash tells a tale of its own,
In the dance of the waves, all mischief is grown.

And as dawn awakens, the magic takes flight,
Silvery flickers will vanish from sight.
Yet whispers remain in the bubbles that gleam,
Of the mischief and magic, alive in a dream.

Elysian Dreams in Marine Palettes

In the quiet of dawn, hues gentle and fair,
Elysian dreams float on the salt-kissed air.
With strokes of the sea, in blues and in gold,
A palette of wonders, surreal and bold.

Coral gardens bloom, a masterpiece grows,
Pastels of the reef like soft-spoken prose.
Each sway of the waves, a brush to define,
The beauty of life where the sun starts to shine.

Oysters hide jewels in soft silty beds,
While starfish unfold their delicate spreads.
In every small creature, an artist's sweet claim,
Painting the ocean, an ethereal frame.

Beneath the surface, tranquility reigns,
Where echoes of dreams swirl in the currents' veins.
And dolphins leap high in a splash of pure bliss,
In this Elysium, the world feels like this.

As the sun dips low, and shadows take form,
In the heart of the ocean, tranquility's warm.
Elysian dreams live where the deep waters dwell,
In the palette of life, all stories to tell.

Dances in a Crystal Casket

In a chamber softly lit,
Crystal shadows sway and flit.
Elegance in every twirl,
Magic wraps around the world.

Whispers trace the turning glass,
Moments held that time won't pass.
Every dance a secret told,
In the gleam of dreams unrolled.

Laughter sparkles in the air,
Chasing thoughts beyond compare.
With each note, the heart takes flight,
Lost in soft, enchanted night.

Moonlight weaves a silver thread,
Through the stories softly said.
In this casket, dreams reside,
Where the forgotten joys abide.

When the clock begins to chime,
Graceful echoes blend with time.
In the end, as shadows part,
Dance remains within the heart.

The Pearl's Whisper in the Abyss

Beneath waves of deep, dark blue,
Secrets murmur, ancient, true.
In the depths, a pearl does gleam,
Guarding sorrows, hopes, and dream.

Tales of sailors lost at sea,
Echo softly, hauntingly.
With each wave that crashes near,
The abyss holds what we most fear.

Moonlit ripples dance and play,
Guided by the light of day.
Every shimmer calls our name,
In the depths, there lies no shame.

Crimson tides and quiet night,
The pearl's glow, a gentle light.
Whispers rising, flowing free,
In the cold embrace of sea.

So we listen to the lore,
In the depths, there's so much more.
Each whisper, a heart's request,
In the abyss, dreams find rest.

Uriana's Dream on the Beach

Uriana walks where soft waves kiss,
The shoreline holds her secret wish.
Grains of sand slip through her hand,
As she gazes across the land.

Beneath a sky of shades so bright,
She dreams of magic, pure delight.
Each ripple tells a story old,
Of adventures yet untold.

Seagulls cry a lullaby sweet,
As she dances on the heat.
Her laughter mingles with the breeze,
A joyful song among the trees.

At twilight, colors blend and flow,
Painting dreams in evening's glow.
Inheriting the stars above,
Uriana spins in waves of love.

Her spirit roams the endless shore,
Where sea and dreams forever soar.
With every rise and fall of tide,
Her heart finds home; there is no divide.

The Soft Gaze of Ocean's Lore

Beneath the sun's warm, gentle gaze,
The ocean speaks in endless ways.
With every swell and every sigh,
Its stories ripple, never die.

In every drop, a world concealed,
Secrets longing to be revealed.
Through salt and spray, the wisdom flows,
Of ancient tides and time's soft woes.

Idyllic shores where dreams align,
The ocean whispers, so divine.
Her voice a symphony of grace,
With every wave, a soft embrace.

Reflecting hues of dusk and dawn,
The soft gaze beckons, calling on.
Beneath the surface, tales abound,
In the heart of waves, truth is found.

So sail upon its vast expanse,
Join in the timeless dance.
For in the ocean's tender lore,
We find ourselves forevermore.

Beneath the Glimmering Surface

Beneath the waves, a world unfolds,
Secrets whispered, treasures untold,
Silver fish dance, in shimmering light,
Magic abounds, both day and night.

Coral castles, vibrant and bright,
Guarded by creatures, hidden from sight,
Each ripple sings a story so old,
In the depths, the brave hearts feel bold.

A gentle current, a soft embrace,
Guides the lost to a safer place,
Beneath the glimmer, shadows may play,
Luring the dreamers, who've drifted away.

Oceans of wonders, uncharted and vast,
Echos of moments, forever to last,
In this realm, time dances and sways,
Eclipsing the worries of dreary days.

With every tide, a tale to write,
Beneath the stars, the sea feels right,
In enchanted waters, hearts intertwine,
Beneath the surface, legends align.

Constellations in the Foam

In swirling depths, where foam does play,
Constellations burst, at the end of day,
Stars reflected, in a frothy embrace,
Wishes take flight, lost in the race.

The ocean hums, with a voice so sweet,
Echoes of laughter, where wave and shore meet,
Each crest a canvas, painted in dreams,
Where hope flows freely, or so it seems.

With a gentle splash, the night draws near,
Whispers of magic, drift close to the ear,
In each little bubble, a universe waits,
As foam connects hearts, through inviting gates.

Travelers gather, under moon's soft glow,
Guided by constellations, weaving below,
Waves carry stories, both old and brand new,
In silvery ripples, the night feels so true.

As stars shimmer brightly, in the tide's quiet dance,
The sea cradles dreams, as if in a trance,
For in every wave, a tale is reborn,
A cosmic reminder, with each radiant dawn.

A Siren's Puzzle of the Deep

In shadows deep, where the mermaids sing,
Lurks a riddle, with a haunting ring,
Sirens weave spells, with voices like gold,
Secrets entwined, in tales of old.

Flashes of beauty, in the moon's soft gaze,
Luring the sailors, caught in a haze,
A puzzle of whispers, that coaxes you close,
As the ocean's heart, begins to doze.

In currents of magic, the answers hide,
Within the echoes, where the lost reside,
With shimmering scales and a beguiling smile,
They weave their enchantment, beguile for a while.

But tread with caution, for secrets may bind,
The puzzle of love, not easily defined,
In serenades sweet, danger conceals,
For the depths of desire, the sea reveals.

So listen intently, to the siren's call,
For truths may be shrouded, and shadows may fall,
Amidst the waves, where dreams start to seep,
Awake your heart, from the depths of the deep.

The Melody of Whispering Currents

Whispering currents, soft and low,
Sing of distant lands, where legends grow,
A lullaby flows, through the rocks and the sand,
Carrying tales, from a faraway land.

With each gentle surge, the water will flow,
Cascading secrets, of high and of low,
Melodies mingle, in perfect refrain,
Dancing together, through joy and through pain.

From tranquil bays, to turbulent seas,
The heartbeat of water, whispers with ease,
It tells of the wanderers, hearts full of dreams,
Where adventure begins, or so it seems.

The tide sings a story, woven in time,
Each wave a stanza, each splash a rhyme,
Under starlit skies, let your spirit be free,
With the melody born, from the depths of the sea.

In the hush of the night, close your eyes tight,
Feel the embrace of the moon's silver light,
For in the deep magic, the currents confide,
The whispers of water, where wonders abide.

Ballad of the Abyssal Depths

In the depths where shadows dance,
Whispers of the ocean's trance.
Creatures lurking, secrets kept,
In the silence, mysteries wept.

Forgotten ships on silted beds,
Echoes of the sailors' dreads.
Crimson corals, nature's art,
Guarding tales of lost heart.

Currents weave a ghostly song,
Tales of right and tales of wrong.
Beneath the waves, the lost do dwell,
In the ocean, there's a spell.

Stars above but dark below,
In the depths, no light shall glow.
Yet in the dark, a beauty lies,
Written in the siren's sighs.

Bravery, a fleeting spark,
In the heart of oceans dark.
Adventures call from watery graves,
For the bold, the daring waves.

Secrets Entwined in Seafoam

Whispers rise with foamy kiss,
Tales of fortune, love, and bliss.
Beneath the froth, the stories sleep,
In the blue and depths so deep.

Mermaids' laughter, soft and low,
Guides the lost where currents flow.
Shells and stones that softly sing,
Of the marvels that tides bring.

Glimmering threads of light and shade,
In the brine, old dreams are laid.
Jewel-toned fish in gentle sway,
Guard the secrets of the bay.

Moonlight dances on the crest,
Inviting souls to seek their quest.
In the ebb and flow of time,
Lies the heart of every rhyme.

Sailing ships with hopes anew,
Cast their nets in shimmering blue.
Devotion found on ocean's breath,
Anchored firm despite the depth.

The Deep's Rhapsody

Dancing waves beneath the glow,
Weaving tales of ebb and flow.
In the silence, music plays,
Echoing through endless days.

Fathoms deep, the secrets blend,
Where the sea and dreams descend.
Seaglass glimmers, memories bright,
In the hush of approaching night.

Songs of whales in solemn verse,
Resonate, disperse the curse.
Joy and sorrow intertwined,
In each note, a heart defined.

Compass hearts lost in the tide,
Follow where the currents guide.
Every crest and every trough,
Promises that can't be scoffed.

Endless rhythms, pure and real,
In the depths, they softly heal.
Tales of old shall forever stay,
In the deep's rhapsody, they play.

Cascading Tides of Forgotten Memories

Waves embrace the sandy shore,
Echoes whisper evermore.
In the ripples, memories gleam,
Drifting softly like a dream.

Once upon a silvered tide,
Lies a story deep inside.
Released from time, they come alive,
In the ocean's heart, they strive.

From the depths, a voice will rise,
Carrying the weight of sighs.
Cascading tides, both wild and free,
Dance with ghosts of memory.

Concealed laughter, tears like pearls,
In the sea, the past unfurls.
Whispered names upon the breeze,
Caught in starlit memories.

With each wave, the shadows part,
Revealing tales of every heart.
Tides will turn, yet time shall flow,
To the depths where love will grow.

Misty Reverie of the Nautilus

In a shell of silver, deep and wide,
Secrets of the ocean gently bide.
Whispers of the waves, a haunting song,
Where dreams of sailors drift along.

Curtains of fog weave tales untold,
As the boat sails by, daring and bold.
Mysteries awaken in the twilight's breath,
Life and death dance, entwined beneath.

Souls of the deep gaze from afar,
Guiding the way like a distant star.
With every ripple, hope's echoes grow,
In the stillness, enchanted waters flow.

Luminous creatures 'neath the glistening tide,
Guardian spirits of those who glide.
Through the mist, the heart finds peace,
As the stories of the ocean never cease.

Sailing through realms where echoes remain,
In the nautilus, knowledge uncontained.
In every whisper, the sea's dear lore,
In the heart of the mariner forevermore.

Currents of Passion

In the rush of the river, a spirit flows,
Carving the valleys where wildflower grows.
Life's sweet currents call soft and low,
In the dance of the water, pure emotions glow.

With every wave comes a song anew,
Love's ardor ignites, fierce and true.
On the surface, ripples of dreams collide,
Passion's embrace, a wondrous tide.

Under the moon's watchful, silvery glance,
The heart beckons forth, lost in its dance.
In flowing whispers, strength intertwines,
As the river flows on, love defines.

Spirals of tenderness eddy and swirl,
Euphoria lifts as the echoes unfurl.
In the depths where joy's secrets lie,
Currents of passion forever will sigh.

So let the waters of time gently weave,
A tapestry of love, weaves heartstrings believe.
As night kisses day, each pulse the same,
In the flow of life, we kindle the flame.

Swaying Softly

In the forest's embrace, where shadows play,
The leaves dance softly, night turns to day.
Gentle breezes hum a tune,
Cradling the earth beneath the moon.

With every sway, stories emerge,
Whispers of nature, a sacred surge.
Occasional branches twirl and sigh,
In harmony's rhythm, they reach for the sky.

Rustling secrets hide in the green,
In the swell of the wind, magic is seen.
Softly the heart aligns with each sound,
In nature's ballet, a solace profound.

From blades of grass to the towering spruces,
The air filled with laughter, no heart refuses.
Beneath the vast arch of twinkling light,
Nature's embrace, a true delight.

So let us sway, our spirits aligned,
In the melody's grip, we become entwined.
With nature's soft touch, peace finds its way,
As we dance through the night, where dreams lay.

Starlit Dances on the Surface

Under the canopy where dreams reside,
Stars twinkle brightly, secrets confide.
The water reflects their ancient glow,
In the still of the night, the world seems slow.

A silver sheen glimmers, playful and light,
Each ripple a shimmer in the embrace of night.
Footsteps of starlight dance on the waves,
Whispers of wishes the ocean saves.

It's here we wander, lost and free,
Embraced by the cosmos, the sea, and the lea.
With each breath, the universe blends,
In the beauty of stillness, our spirit mends.

As laughter weaves through the cool night air,
The surface shimmers with magic so rare.
In the twilight, we find our grace,
In starlit dances, lost in time and space.

So let us sway where dreams coalesce,
Amongst twinkling jewels, we find our rest.
In the night's tender hush, we are free,
As starlit dances reveal the sea.

The Serenity of Sunlit Doldrums

In stillness, the ocean breathes soft and slow,
Beneath the sun's warmth, peace starts to flow.
No storms to disturb, just a tranquil embrace,
In golden glow, we find our place.

Gentle waves whisper secrets of time,
Caressing the shores in rhythm and rhyme.
Here, dreams drift like clouds in the sky,
In the sunlit doldrums, where spirits fly.

A moment of calm in the heart of the sea,
Where hearts beat as one, wild and free.
Every ripple tells stories of old,
In the arms of the sun, a warmth to hold.

As horizons stretch wide, filled with light,
We gather our hopes, let go of the night.
In the glow of the sun, serenity reigns,
And love blooms eternal, as joy never wanes.

So here we shall linger, in the gentle sway,
Finding solace in colors that brighten our day.
Under the heavens' unyielding grace,
In sunlit doldrums, we've found our place.

www.ingramcontent.com/pod-product-compliance
Ingram Content Group UK Ltd.
Pitfield, Milton Keynes, MK11 3LW, UK
UKHW021518280125
4335UKWH00036B/910